The cave

AF624485

H. H.

BookLeaf Publishing

Presentation by *BookLeaf Publishing*

Web: www.bookleafpub.com

E-mail: info@bookleafpub.com

ISBN: 9789357212373

First edition 2023

DEDICATION

This book is dedicated to anyone who is striving for a better Dunya and a beautiful Akhirah.

ACKNOWLEDGEMENT

Thank you to everyone who contributed to this book by telling me about your favourite Ayah from the Quran. This book would not have been possible without you and your support. May Allah reward you infinitely.

Thank you for deciding to read my book and making my dreams come true.

PREFACE

IWhen this opportunity presented itself, I thought and thought about the poetry I would write. Maybe I was overthinking it to the point where I wouldn't be able to write. Despite it all, I did manage to open my laptop and type even with my hands shaking and heart hammering. This book was written on the bus, in countless coffee shops on my local high street, at the local library and in the depths of the night. I struggled at first, but the more I tried the easier it became to write. Over time it became my secret sanctuary that forced me to re-evaluate everything in this life and contemplate the afterlife. Just like Muhammed (PBUH) used to in the cave of Hira.

57:4

You can't put your pain into words.
I understand.
It happens.
There is no way you can think of to heal the
ache.
So, believe and prostrate because
He is with you wherever you are.

28:24

Remember the words
My Lord I am truly in need of any good you send down to me
Remember them
in sadness,
in grief,
in anxiousness,
in every uncertainty.

8:46

It seems like every time I take a step forward
life drags me two steps back.
So I wait until I can heal and begin to walk again
Indeed Allah is with the patient.

10:65

Do not let them tell you that you are not enough
Do not let them tell you that you are not
beautiful
Do not let them tell you that you are not
intelligent
Do not let them tell you that you are not sincere
Do not let them tell you that you are not kind
Do not let them tell you that you are not brave
Do not let them tell you that you are worthless
Do not let their words sadden you

9:14

My mother always said that breaking someone's
heart is the only sin that Allah will never forgive
you for.
When I asked her why she said
the heart is too fragile
it does not just break it shatters
and the pain it goes through is not visible to the
naked eye
no one knows how to pick up the pieces and put
them back together again
but despite it all you have to be patient and have
faith because ultimately
Allah will soothe the hearts of those who
believe.

2:263

They will ask why you did not punish those that wronged you
and every single time
the answer will be
because a kind word and forgiveness are better.

20:46

When the loneliness is too much
Fear not! Allah is always with you.
How beautiful to think,
that the creation is alone with the creator
doing what they were designed to do
just like our Prophet in the cave of Hira
in complete solitude.

39:53

Every single sinner knows that your bad deeds could reach the mountains and still you do not despair in the mercy of Allah.

2:45

Seek help with patience and prayer.
No matter who you are,
where you are
raise your hands and make Dua.
The trials that are breaking you today
are the ones that are making your mansions
in the afterlife.

8:30

Every single moment in life is meticulously
planned.
By a much more powerful entity than you.
So, the next time you do not get what you want
understand that it was never written for you in
the first place
because Allah is the best of planners.

15:9

Allah says that he is closer to man than his
jugular vein.
Every second he allows the blood to flow in
between the brain and the heart
it reminds us of our insignificance in this holy
life and how close he is to us
yet why does he feel so far away in our darkest
moments?

20:46

Allah tells us in the Quran
Do not be afraid, I am with you all the time
listening and seeing.
So even when the battles inside you threaten to
tear you apart
and there is no one to hold you together
He will.
Every single time.

19:31

Praying Fajr in the mosque is a blessing.
Praying Dhuhr at work is a blessing.
Praying Asar in the park is a blessing.
Praying Maghrib at the beach at sunset is a blessing.
Praying Isha in the comfort of your own home is a blessing.

Every moment spent on this planet praising Allah is a beautiful blessing and I know he made me blessed wherever I am.

14:34

If you begin counting the blessings of Allah
never will you be able to count them.
Not even an hour, a day, a week, a month, a year,
a decade, a century or a millennium.

55:60

Building a water well. Planting a tree. Donating a wheelchair. Gifting someone The Holy Quran. A smile. Every act of charity. Serving your parents. Spread knowledge. Visiting the sick. Love your neighbours. Feed the poor. Take care of the orphans. Don't get angry. Be gentle. Love wholeheartedly. Be good to your spouse. Pray on time. Speak softly.Pray Tahajjud. Keep your fasts.
Is the reward for good anything but good?

93:7

The moment when he found you lost and guided you was the moment that everything made complete sense.

23:115

Whenever the feeling of worthlessness
overcomes you think of the ayah
Did you think we created you without any
purpose?
because you were placed in this world to hope,
to strive, to make all of your dreams come true
and so much more.

2:286

We have to keep reminding each other
Throughout every hardship
Allah will not burden a soul beyond that it can bare.

www.ingramcontent.com/pod-product-compliance
Lightning Source LLC
Chambersburg PA
CBHW051720130826
49812CB00034B/1272
9789357212373